Freedom Here & Now

libertysavard.com

Freedom Here & Now

Liberty Savard

Bridge-Logos *Publishers*

Gainesville, Florida 32614 USA

Freedom Here & Now

Copyright © 2000 by Liberty Savard
Library of Congress Catalog Card Number: Pending
International Standard Book Number: 0-88270-842-2

Bridge-Logos *Publishers*

P.O. Box 141630
Gainesville, FL 32614, USA
http://www.bridgelogos.com

DEDICATION

I dedicate this book to all those who reached out and asked the tough and painful questions . . .hoping for answers.

Bless you and thank you!

TABLE OF CONTENTS

INTRODUCTION

Nearly 2000 years ago, Matthew wrote that Jesus said He was giving the Keys of the Kingdom to His people (16:19, 18:18). Then Jesus added these promises: *"Whatsoever you bind on earth will be bound in heaven, and whatsoever you loose on earth will be loosed in heaven"* (Matthew 16:19). Here are powerful prayer principles that will bring things on earth into alignment with God's already established will in heaven. In the Lord's Prayer (Matthew 6:10; Luke 11:2), Jesus prayed to the Father, *"Thy will be done on earth as it is in heaven."*

Many Hebrew and Greek words for "bind" and "binding" have positive meanings—tie, put oneself under obligation to, weave together, heal, undergird, hold, persuade, and cause fragmented pieces to coalesce and become one whole again. I believe this is a far more exciting and positive use of this powerful key than the tying up of evil spirits.

The word "loose" in the original Greek, *luo,* (and companion words *rhegnumi* and *agnumi*) mean untie, break up, destroy, dissolve, melt, put off, wreck, crack to sunder by separation of the parts, shatter into minute fragments, disrupt, lacerate, convulse with spasms, break forth, burst, rend, tear up. These are strong words that a determined prayer warrior can accomplish great things with!

In J. B. Phillips' introduction to Dr. Alfred Marshall's Interlinear New Testament, Phillips states he was quite pleased that Dr. Marshall had not missed the peculiar Greek construction of Matthew 16:19. Phillips said this verse was "not a celestial endorsement that God would bind and loose in heaven whatever we bound and loosed on earth." Rather, these were our means of coming into agreement with already established heavenly purposes.

These powerful Keys of the Kingdom are our means of coming into agreement with God as we pray that His already established will in heaven be manifested on earth.

The <u>key of binding</u> that Christ has given to His people is the:

1. **steadying,**

2. **stabilizing,**

3. **seat belt, and**

4. **safety harness key.**

As God's children, we can bind our wills to the will of God, our minds to the mind of Christ, and ourselves to the fullness of the truth of His Word. One of the meanings of the word **bind** is to <u>put oneself under obligation</u> to someone (or some thing). I really like the idea of having a scriptural/spiritual power key to use in prayer when I need to put my sometimes unruly will under obligation to God's will!

This key of binding will snug you up close and personal to God for perhaps the first clear look you have ever had regarding His will for your life. A one time prayer does not keep you there,

> *however. As long as your soul is still*
> *unsurrendered to God in any area, it will*
> *continue to try to distract you from pursuing*
> *God's will.*

So, what good does it do to use this key if it is not a permanent solution to our souls' willfulness? I'm glad you asked. Your unsurrendered soul is always working to distract you from God, whether you bind yourself to God's will or not. There is always a fight going on within you over the choices your self-will wants to make. When the binding and loosing keys bring God's power into the fight your soul is waging for control, your soul begins to lose the ground it has held.

The Kingdom <u>key of loosing</u> is the:

1. **self-surgery on the soul,**

2. **severing personal bondages,**

3. **slashing wrong patterns of thinking, and**

4. **spiritual warfare key.**

Loosing is a powerful prayer key for cutting the ties to the clutter your unsurrendered soul still clings to. This prayer key can rid you of present clutter and prevent reattachments of former clutter (old bondages, bad attitudes, etc.). It will clear out the old junk your mind loves to feed on and the grave clothes your soul tries to drape you with.

Loosing prayers also wreak havoc with and cause spiritual terrorism on evil spirits, and loosing prayers destroy stronghold doors that the enemy accesses to harass you. That little nugget is worth the reading of this whole book. Think about this natural example. If you had intruders constantly coming into your house, what would you want most?

1. **To be able to bind the intruders up and leave them laying around, bound, on the ground?**

2. **To be able to tear up and demolish (loose) whatever was holding the doors of your house open (strongholds) and permanently stop the intruders' means of entry?**

This is sort of a "well, duh" question, isn't it? Yet binding evil spirits is exactly what many in the Church have been trying to teach us for years. It may have served some purpose, but who in the Church today can say that it has had a permanent effect on keeping Satan out of our lives?

Binding evil spirits is never effective if you don't deal with the doors of access in the soul. Besides, there are more evil spirits available to harass you than you have time to bind anyway. Trying to use that means of defense is like mopping up around an overflowing toilet without ever turning off the inflowing water! I'll deal with closing the open doors later.

Our minds have carefully filed our wrong mind sets, unforgiveness, desires for revenge, and other ugly attitudes associated with our inability to understand why hard things happened to us. These memories, together with neglect and lack in our early lives, become the sources of the pain still throbbing in our souls today.

> *The memories of these past issues are still so real to some of us that we often lose all perspective of the fact that they actually occurred years earlier.*

The physical fact of the actual abuse may be long over, but the memories are securely locked in the vault of *The First Federal Memory Bank of My Pain*. There the unsurrendered soul carefully tends to them, creatively refining and retooling them to its advantage, while keeping them on artificial life support. If only we could grasp the fact that these memories are the only remaining power our former traumas have over us. Until we do, our unsurrendered souls will continue to cause us to live as if our worst times are still burning and scorching areas of our lives today.

> *The unsurrendered soul's control is based upon its power to both protect (through strongholds) and retrieve (through flashbacks) all of the fear, pain, and humiliation from our past experiences. With interactive graphics, living color, Dolby sound, and scratch-and-sniff patches included!*

Christians trapped in this mode of soulish bondage live uneasily under the threat of traumatic memories flashing to the surface of their minds at any moment.

The defense system our souls build and use are constructed of strongholds which are the:

1. **arguments,**
2. **reasonings,**
3. **rationalizations,**
4. **justifications, and**
5. **denial**

that we use to explain and defend:

1. **why we are still the way we are,**
2. **why we can't love others,**
3. **why we can't forgive others' mistakes,**
4. **why we want to get even, and**
5. **why we live so far beneath our heritage as children of God.**

The strongholds protect these lies through reasonings and rationalizations that:

1. **we have been hurt too much to change,**

2. **we have been hurt too much to love,**

3. **we have been hurt too much to forgive,**

4. **we deserve to see others suffer for what they did to us, and**

5. **we are doing the best we can with the burden we have to bear.**

Then the biggest lie of all surfaces:

God knows what we've been through, and He understands why we are the way we are. Thank heavens He doesn't expect us to do the "heavy lifting" of obedience and forgiveness and surrender like He does other Christians who haven't suffered like we have!

This may sound cruel to some, but living under these lies **is much crueler**. These self-deceptions must be destroyed, smashed, and shattered, or the Christian trapped in them will never break free! God knows exactly what we've been through and it has not exceeded what others have experienced. Paul tells us that, *"No test that comes your way is beyond the course of what others have had to face"* (1 Corinthians 10:13, *The Message*).

Only as our stronghold thinking is demolished through prayer can God move into the inner chambers of our souls. There He will meet our deepest needs, heal our oldest hurts, and resolve our worst fears. When we give Him voluntary access to do that, He will then fill the hidden chambers of our souls with light and grace and mercy and love!

As believers in Christ, our spirits are born again, but our souls are fighting for **control of** our lives. This is the ongoing conflict within us. As I have used the binding and loosing prayers over my former muddled thinking, traumatic memories, and soulish defenses, I have recognized something. These prayers have been more effective in a relatively short period of time than all of the other prayers I have prayed since becoming a Christian in 1972!

One benefit of receiving healing in your soul is that you realize you can look beyond yourself. You begin to recognize that you may have something very useful to share with other hurting people. These keys offer a powerful way of praying for others.

Some people struggle with praying to bind another person's will to the will of God, even calling it witchcraft. That is simple enough to refute by asking the question: what is the goal of witchcraft? It is always to gain power and benefit from controlling another person's will. If you pray and bind someone's will to the will of God, where is your gain of power or benefit?

Binding peoples' wills to the will of God neither controls nor removes their right to choose. This praying act of love only snugs them up close and personal to His will until they choose to pull away.

But <u>however brief that snugged-up moment is</u>, they may get their very first glimpse of the goodness and love inherent in God's will and plans for their lives. Especially as you continue to bind them to His will again and again.

The content of this book is taken from my question and answer ministry on the Liberty Savard Ministries website (http://www.libertysavard.com). Anonymity has been assured by modifications of relationships, facts, details, etc. There have been so many painful questions pour into our office each week by e-mail, as well as by phone, fax, and snail mail. I believe the Lord has anointed me to answer these often hard questions.

This mini-book is the beginning of a series of collections of some of the answers that I believe Christians are searching for. May you take heart that you are not the only one with questions. There are effective prayer principles to cut away the grave clothes of your past that create the bondages of your present. You can be free to embrace your future!

I am praying that you will find answers in this book and be assured that it is time to claim your *Freedom Here & Now*!

1

FREEDOM FROM STRONGHOLDS

Question (Part 1): *How do I know if my binding and loosing prayers are pulling down my strongholds?*

Liberty's Answer: Personal strongholds are the arguments, logic, and reasoning you use to justify your beliefs and your behaviors (Thayer's Greek-English Lexicon). You will know your strongholds are starting to come down as you see your reactions to other people and to uncomfortable circumstances <u>change</u>. There is only one way to know if you are growing spiritually. That is when you deal with difficult people or walk through hard spots that used to make you crash and burn, and you walk right past them with little or no reaction.

As your strongholds begin to quietly crumble or crash and tumble, you will find yourself walking through edgy situations with peace. You will be concerned with getting on with more important things instead of going into meltdown over less important things.

Question (Part 2): *Is there a time line to follow or to expect when pulling down strongholds?*

Liberty's Answer: No, because each person brings such a different mixture of experience, memories, and deceptions into the equation of stronghold building. How you are applying these principles is another factor. Memorizing all of the inspirational truth in the world is useless unless you <u>apply it in your life</u>. Prayer is the application of the truths of the Keys of the Kingdom.

Some people faithfully read the prayers every day. That is better than ignoring the principles, but prayers to tear down strongholds should be <u>prayed</u>. This requires focus upon and attention to each word. This kind of focused prayer will be strongly resisted by your soul as it realizes that its things held dear and its half-truths so cherished are being seriously challenged.

Question (Part 3): *How long did it take you to pull down the strongholds in your soul, and how did you know when you were completely free?*

Liberty's Answer: It took me quite a while to make some serious inroads, and I'm not completely free yet. But I'm getting so free, it sometimes scares me! In the beginning, I had quite a struggle with my initial attempts to pull down my strongholds. I had no one who would agree with me in these prayers, no books to read to see if I was doing it right, no web site to e-mail questions to, and nothing to check myself against except my own experiences after praying. And I had to keep trying to use the stream of new input coming from the Holy Ghost.

It was hard to hear the Holy Ghost clearly at first, because I was not used to being on my own with Him. I was not used to searching out my own understanding of God's revelation. I had always been comfortable being spoon fed by pastors and spiritual teachers. My soul pitched a fit as I began to challenge it, throwing up all kinds of static between my pitiful little spiritual earphones and God's incoming messages. Nevertheless, I was determined to go for whatever God was trying to tell me.

Question (Part 4): *How can I run to the finish line against these strongholds and against the OLD MAN when I can't even see a finish line to run to?*

Liberty's Answer: Ah, but that is what faith is all about—grabbing hold of the promise that there is an exciting finish line and you will get to it—and then just running with abandon and love. This requires trust and confidence in God. That is exactly what faith is—faith is not a force, nor a weapon against Satan, nor a heavenly form of currency to get what you want in prayer. Faith is:

> *Trust and confidence in God's goodness, purposes, and wisdom towards you.*

Faith is taking your marching orders and setting out, believing that God is going to supply whatever you need as you go forth bound to His will. Binding and loosing prayers are about getting to the place where you want only God's will and purposes. This small prayer may give you more understanding as you pray it:

Thank you, dear God, for the Keys of the Kingdom. I am so grateful to have these scriptural/spiritual keys that empower me to overcome my soul's interfering with what my spirit wants to do. I bind my body, soul, and spirit to your will for my life. I bind my soul's reactions to my spirit's actions. My spirit draws directly from the Spirit of the Creator who created me! How awesome.

I loose all wrong patterns of thinking, and I loose the agitation and anxiety my soul is churning up. I loose my soul's hold on the wrong attitudes that keep trying to surface in me, and I throw them to you. I will trust you, for I know that confidence in you will never be disappointed. I ask for your peace, your grace, and your view of my eternal purposes in your Kingdom. I ask for more of you, Lord. Amen.

2

FREEDOM HOW SOON?

Question: *After I've started binding and loosing, when can I expect to see results?*

Liberty's Answer: Some people feel a release of the control issues in their souls immediately after praying their first binding and loosing prayers. For others, it may take a few days of praying this way. Some people, whose souls have built up elaborate self-protection systems, may have to pray for a longer period of time to see results.

Every time these prayers are prayed, however, there is a tearing down of some stronghold walls within the person praying them. Paul was talking to born-again believers in Corinth when he told them to pull down their strongholds and every "high thing" exalting itself between them and knowledge of God. Those "high things" are the self-defense systems, self-denial, and self-deception that the unsurrendered soul uses to try to cover over its toxic waste pits. These are the accumulated deposits of pain and bitterness and unforgiveness it still clings to, wanting to get even.

> *Discovering and placing blame might seem logical to your soul's desire for revenge, but it will never heal you.*

Anything your soul establishes by choices of your will is going to remain firmly in place until you tear it down. Binding your will to God's will and loosing your wrong thinking will pull down strongholds guarding the areas of your soul that most need God's help.

> *I bind myself to your timing, Lord. I know I move in a human understanding of time that pressures my ability to see your ongoing work in my life.*

My impatience also crowds my ability to make godly choices. But your eternal clock has no hands, for you do not exist in the framework of time as your children perceive it. Help me, Lord, to move at your chosen pace for my life. Help me to move quickly when you want me to and to stand and wait when you want me to.

I loose all preconceived ideas I have about what you are doing, what you should do, how you should do it, and WHEN you should do it. I bind my will to its obligation to your will, and I bind my mind to agreement with the mind of Christ. Help me to hold still under the Master workings of your mighty hands until my healing is complete. Amen.

3

FREEDOM FROM INNER TURMOIL

Question: *I've been a born again Christian for about six years. I recently browsed through your web site and read your article concerning the unsurrendered soul. I believe that is what my problem is. Right now Satan has a deep stronghold on my life. I need to be delivered from lust, adulterous thoughts, depression, fear, and financial bondage. I've been struggling in these areas for years and I want to be free. I want to serve God and do right, but it seems like something just won't let me.*

Liberty's Answer: That "something" is your unsurrendered soul, and you can definitely do something

11

about it! Christians' mental and emotional struggles come from their unsurrendered souls' unmet needs, unhealed hurts, and unresolved issues. Wrong thought patterns and ugly mind sets develop from confusion and anger over why these hurts were inflicted upon them in the first place.

> ***When wounded angry people become Christians and then learn that God was always with them, even during their worst times, this information can create great conflict within the human soul. Since we know we are not supposed to blame God (for not stopping the trauma), we begin to stuff our hard questions and unresolved issues. Then we pretend that we know God loves us and everything is just wonderful, thank you very much!***

Unfortunately, our Christian pretense that we're just fine does little to deal with the ugly questions and growing anger that keeps rolling around inside of us. We find ourselves building strongholds in our souls to try to hide such ungodly feelings. Understanding that you have done this will help you close open doors in your soul that have allowed the enemy to further poison your feelings. Understanding this will also simultaneously open up your buried pain and questions to God for healing. Praying the binding and loosing prayers can make your soul allow this to happen.

Satan does not build the strongholds in your life, but he will certainly pressure you to build them and then take advantage of the access they offer him. The Amplified Bible gives a very good example of a stronghold door of access birthed out of disobedience to God's clear commandment in Ephesians 4:26: *"When angry, do not sin; do not ever let your wrath—your exasperation, your fury or indignation—last until the sun goes down."* Disobedience to this verse can be reversed by acknowledging the sin of deliberately holding onto your anger, repenting for having done so (turning away from any desire to repeat the act), and then asking the Lord for forgiveness.

Verse 27 warns us of the consequences of disobeying verse 26 and then trying to rationalize and justify our belief that we really had every right to be angry. The warning is clear: *"Leave no (such) room or foothold for the devil—give no opportunity to him."*

Question (Part 2): *Right now I'm out of fellowship with God. I want to know what His will is for my life, but I just can't hear His voice. I want to walk in the Spirit and live a victorious life, but I can't get past these strongholds. I have a problem trying to pray and getting into the Word of God. I don't want to continue on like this. I really need to be delivered and set free.*

Liberty's Answer: You are crying out for this freedom and opposing the receiving of it at the same time. No wonder you feel helpless and hopeless! Nevertheless, Christ has always been and still is offering help to you. You have not understood that you are blocking your own divine help. Not only can you hope to be free, but you can also learn how to cooperate with and speed up getting free! Read on.

Question (Part 3): *I've had many prophetic words spoken about the calling of God on me. Why can't I start fulfilling these prophecies? If God called me into the ministry, why does it seem like I'm in total despair (financially, spiritually, emotionally)? I want to do the will of God, but I'm weak in my spirit.*

14

Liberty's Answer: I have good news for you!

Your born-again spirit is not weak! Neither is it fearful, needy, or any other negative thing. Most exciting of all, it is no longer a spiritual orphan. By the blood of Jesus, it has been linked to the Spirit of your Creator and—Important Announcement Here!!!—your born-again spirit is just fine.

Now your unsurrendered soul is a different matter. That rebellious rascal is scrambling madly around trying to block any natural outflow of the spiritual input that your spirit has received from God. This is the exhausting inner activity causing you to feel weak. God has a wonderful plan for you that began before you were knit together in your mother's womb. He's just had a problem getting you to make room—in your mind, will, and emotions—to receive it all.

God's will and purposes for your life are laid down in heaven somewhat like a "railroad track." Your soul has been like a wayward little locomotive chugging off into the ditch, getting lost in the forest, and dragging itself through the desert. When you begin to realize that your

15

spirit man has been given a map to bring God's will (your destiny "track" that has always been laid down in heaven) together with your will (the inferior track that is entrenched in your soul), life will start getting very exciting for you!

> *For we are God's (own) handiwork (His workmanship), recreated in Christ Jesus, (born anew) that we may do those good works which God predestined (planned beforehand) for us, (taking paths which He prepared ahead of time) that we should walk in them—living the good life which He prearranged and made ready for us to live*

(Ephesians 2:10, Amplified).

Your destiny has already been all planned out and set in place for you in heaven. Yahoo! And here's the really exciting part—your born-again spirit is completely encoded with all that you will ever need to fulfill it. This is the same principle, except on an infinitely smaller scale, as a tiny apple seed being encoded with everything it will ever need to fulfill its destiny of become a giant apple tree bearing sweet fruit!

The Incorruptible Seed of Christ's perfect life was implanted into your spirit at the time of your salvation and rebirth. All that He has for those of us who believe in Him—the gifts of the Spirit, the fruit of the Spirit, power, mercy, grace, and spiritual purpose—is already within you! If you want to talk about a power concept, there's one for sure! Your born-again spirit is "encoded," if you will allow me to use that contemporary term, with every answer and all ability to do what God has called you to do. Your answers and ministry calling and instructions are not out there somewhere in the foggy future—they are already right inside of you. Isn't that something?

You have not realized this because your unsurrendered soul has been blocking these wonderful attributes of Christ from flowing out of your spirit. But you can loose your soul's blocking agendas and get yourself ready for God's agendas!

One more time—the destiny plans for your incredible future are already encoded into that Incorruptible Seed within your born-again spirit **right now**. And, glory to God, these plans do not need any natural resources for fulfillment. So, it doesn't matter if you are not rich. It doesn't matter if you can't write, can't draw, can't act, and can't play the piano! It doesn't matter if you don't have the "perfect" look, weight, height, or voice. You just need to use the Keys of the Kingdom and get rid of all of the imperfect "stuff" you do have, and then let God be God. He'll lift you into your end times messenger position of favor and great influence—just as you are!

> *Your unsurrendered soul is withstanding the breakthroughs you need with God. The Keys of the Kingdom prayer principles can dismantle your soul's interference here and make way for you to receive everything you need. The choice really is up to you!*

If your unsurrendered soul ignores or rebels against hearing from God's Spirit through your spirit, its pain and neediness will increase. Feeling desperate, it will seek ways to comfort and console itself. It will enlist your body's cooperation (wrong mind-body agreement) by sending out wrong signals and misdirectives to pursue external forms of comfort, gratification, and stimulation.

Because of what happened in the Garden of Eden with Adam and Eve, a break was created between the human spirit and the Spirit of God. That means that you and every baby since that time has been born with an orphaned spirit, and:

- **a soul that was dead in trespasses and sin (Ephesians 2:1),**
- **a soul determined to fulfill its own desires of the flesh and the mind (Ephesians 2:3),**
- **a soul that had no hope (Ephesians 2:12),**
- **a soul that was once in complete darkness (Ephesians 5:8).**

In the completely vulnerable, unlearned, inexperienced state of a child's mind, you began to form lifelong beliefs, mind sets, and opinions about yourself, others, and God. And you formed these beliefs about life from the input of parents and authority figures who were born into life in exactly the same circumstances.

Can you see now that you may still be clinging to beliefs that you formed from really wrong input when you were too young to know any better? Would you be willing to consider that you may still have some deception in your soul affecting your desire to trust God today?

> *In the name of Jesus Christ, I bind my body, soul, and spirit to the will and purposes of God. I bind myself to the truth of God. His Word says that I can trust Him in everything, so I bind myself to that truth. I bind myself to an awareness of the power of the blood of Jesus working in my life every day. I bind my mind to the mind of Christ. I need to hear you say you love me, Jesus. I need to hear you're thinking of me right now.*

> *Lord, I want to be free of all the bondage and baggage I've been carrying. I want to be free. I want to set free all of those I have never forgiven, but instead have locked into "prison cells" in my soul. I repent of having these wrong attitudes and thoughts, and I ask you to forgive me for having them. I choose to forgive all those I have felt wronged me. Please forgive them, Lord, bless them, heal them, and help them fulfill the destinies you created them to fulfill.*

In the name of Jesus, I loose the power and the effects of any harsh or hard words (word curses) spoken about me, to me, or by me. I loose any stronghold thinking connected with these wrong words. Please pour out your mercy and grace upon me, Father, for I need it so much. I am going to use the keys of prayer that Jesus gave to me to make room to receive all that you have for me. Amen

Begin to pray the above prayer, and keep asking God to pour grace and mercy and healing into every area of vulnerability you have. ***Shattering Your Strongholds*** will help you understand what you are doing and what to expect in the way of reactions from your unsurrendered soul. God bless you.

4

FREEDOM FROM DEPRESSION

Question: *I was once in the ministry, but turned away from it to pursue another profession which caused a complete break with my relationship with God. After a period of time, I rededicated my life to the Lord and asked Him to forgive me. But He doesn't seem to be answering my prayers anymore.*

I'm staggering under a huge debt load, I distrust everyone (including God), and I'm at my wits end! I thought that when I came back to Him that everything would begin to work out. Now, I'm thinking of just ending it all. Maybe then God will listen.

Liberty's Answer: I have no doubt that your unsurrendered soul believes what you have just said. No wonder it is depressed and desperate! When we are the most desperate, we usually want immediate soulish answers, not His answers. You should be very grateful that God has not answered some of your prayers since you have not been wanting to hear His answers. In love, God withholds answers that would cause us to remain in our misery.

You say you don't trust God any more because He has not answered your prayers. I remember saying that same thing in years past. I've been a Christian since 1972, the first thirteen years of which were frequently awful from my perspective. I tried to outsmart God. I accused Him of being unfaithful to me, and I was constantly complaining to Him and whoever else would listen. It is only by His pure love, grace, and mercy that I wasn't turned into "toast" in those early years of my bumpy relationship with Him.

I believe that we often pray wonderful (highly religious even) prayers asking for what we feel are the only possible solutions to our most pressing situations. Our souls stubbornly conclude that no other answers could exist. Therefore, if God does not answer accordingly, our souls insist that God does not care and cannot be trusted! All the while, God knows that the answers the soul is seeking will only prolong the painful situation. God does not give what the soul wants—the soul does not want what God will give. This is called a standoff, and:

No one ever wins a standoff with God!

You say that you feel that I will just blame your soul for what you are experiencing, and this won't help. What should we blame if the problem really is your soul? You need **to break out of the control it has effected over your life.**

> *You need to loose (cut and sever) the cords of your soul's bondage. This is where the most personally effective power comes into being when you use the binding and loosing principles of prayer (Matthew 16:19)—breaking free of your own soulish bondage.*

You are obviously both intelligent and educated. This is good, but it can complicate your grasp of just how simple

25

the binding and loosing principles are. You will never know how simple, unless you try them.

I have spent the last fifteen years of my ministry learning about the power of the unsurrendered soul. I've done this while living out hard consequences of my own unsurrendered soul's stubbornness, while trying to understand God's revelation of this message. I have committed all that I have studied, learned, practiced, and seen the fruit of, into the three books that make up what I call the *Keys of The Kingdom Trilogy*. There is no practical way I can give you three pills and a "call me in the morning" directive here. You need some serious prayer power to unseat your unsurrendered soul's position in your life and destroy the lies it has been feeding to you. You need to learn how to pray with these divine keys of prayer.

If you choose not to read any of these books, my life won't change. Your life probably won't change, either. There is a strong possibility you will just feel that you are being more ignored than ever by God. Getting back into close relationship with God will come only through obedience and surrender. Unfortunately, the words **obedience and surrender to God** cause your unsurrendered soul to frantically hit the trenches for an all-out war of control. Don't listen to what your soul will try to deceive you with, for you cannot trust what it will tell you right now. Listening to it when it is in battle mode is like asking a compulsive liar if he is telling you the truth!

The human soul is capable of doing __anything__ that it feels will protect its status of running the human life experience.

You say that you don't care anymore and that you are completely disillusioned. You do care, or you wouldn't have written. So let's cut to the chase here about how to get out of your disillusionment mode. The Keys of the Kingdom can open up all of your soulish deceptions like an electric can opener. These prayer principles strip away the smoke and mirrors, satanic deceptions, and religious half-truths in your soul, getting right down to the real sources of its anger, fear, and pain. The end result is that God can then get into your needs and wounds with healing and truth.

When you know you are using something that works and going somewhere that is both spiritually real and permanent—a new determination settles on you. This determination will carry you through when your soul starts kicking and screaming as it senses it is losing its grip on your life. The choice is yours, and I will be praying for you that you make the right one. Stay in touch and let me know how you are doing. At least pray the very simple prayer below for a first step.

Lord, if I'm wrong and my soul has been deceiving me and I have believed it, please forgive me. I now bind my mind to the mind of Christ, and I ask for an infilling of His thoughts. I bind my will to your will, God, and I ask for a new set of life instructions.

I loose all deception, denial, discouragement, depresssion, wrong patterns of thinking, and wrong agreements from myself. I loose the enemy's assignments from my life. I really need to hear you say that there is a Kingdom plan for me to fulfill and that I haven't ruined it. If I really still have a ministry and a divine purpose in life, help me fulfill it, Father God. Amen.

5

FREEDOM FROM ANGER

Question: *I started using your binding and loosing principles about seven months ago and although I do believe that they have worked miracles in my husband's life, I have not found any answers for my outbursts of anger, insecurity, impatience etc. All aspects that you mentioned in your book seem to be pointing to strongholds. I pray and break my strongholds in general every day, but these emotions will not go away, and they are now causing havoc in my life.*

There was a time that the choices I made did not include God's plans, and it caused a lot of pain for a lot of people. I have repented for these wrong choices, but I am wondering if this still has an influence over my life. Could this be the reason for such terrible struggles as I try to get closer to God? Or could it be that I am just not breaking down the right strongholds? If so, how do I know which stronghold to call by what name?

Liberty's Answer: The anger you are feeling has probably been in your soul for a very long time. If it is trying to surface, don't try to stop it. **Let it come out.** Just pray constantly for God's grace and mercy to be upon you and those around you.

> *God has allowed you to loosen enough of your strongholds and self-protection devices that you can no longer control the force of that buried anger. It might not seem so, but this is a good thing!*

Pray intensely with the binding and loosing prayers, **particularly with regard to tearing off everything your soul has used to bury your anger**. I urge you to focus on praying any of the prayers in the *Keys of the Kingdom Trilogy* books you can make time for. Just change the names and pronouns in any of the prayers to make them applicable to yourself. You need to launch a sustained attack on your soul's defense systems.

Particularly pray the Breaking Soul Power prayer on page 30 of *Breaking the Power*. People who have consistently prayed this prayer for at least 30 days have seen massive breakthrough in the powering down of their souls. They have also reported a common phenomenon that the resonating soulish "output" of other angry and irritated souls cause a matching resonance in their souls. I still haven't figured it out completely, I just know I've experienced it, too. Oh, how I wish this had been working in my life in so many past experiences I have had with picking up on group or crowd mentalities!

Your soul is pulling out all the stops against you right now. Bring in bigger fire power with the divine Keys of the Kingdom and end the conflict. There is a particular passage in the *Breaking the Power* (page 30) "speaking-to-your-soul/praying to God prayer" that basically says:

Emotions, forget not how you once reeled between laughter and tears, boldness and fear, hope and despair, affection and anger. You frightened people away from me by either bordering on tears of neediness or outbursts of rage, and then you fed fuel to my feelings of rejection and loneliness within. But now, emotions, you are learning to receive divine peace, to express joy and hope, to respond to the Holy Spirit's lifting power when old, negative feelings try to ascend. I bind you, emotions, to the divine role you are to play in my life: your unique ability to project God's peace and joy and hope to those who do not understand the promises of His Spirit. You bless the Lord, O my soul, and forget not His benefits!

Will, forget not the causes and the battles you used to engage in, always rigidly implacable and unrelenting in your stands. Unrepentant, unbending, unyielding, always unwilling to work with another's ideas, you alienated many. Will, you caused much grief with your stubbornness, resistance, and rebellion to God's ways. But now, my will, you are bound to the will of the Father. You are learning how to be strong, yet flexible; to be right, yet entreatable; to be bold, yet gentle; to be courageous, yet concerned for others. Only the Holy Spirit can perfectly balance each side of these strengths in me. I bind you, will, to the total and complete purposes and plans of the Lord. I bind you to the will of my heavenly Father. Amen.

Don't give up. Don't get discouraged. Get divinely intimate! God wants you to use the Keys of the Kingdom to tear down all of the false defenses you have allowed your soul to erect, voluntarily making yourself vulnerable to His healing power. That is intimacy with God.

6

FREEDOM PRAYERS FOR LOVED ONES IN HOMOSEXUALITY

Question: *How do my husband and I pray for his niece who is a lesbian? My husband's side of the family thinks her problem is genetic and can't be helped. Some of the other relatives think that homosexuality is wrong, but they don't have any Christian perspective of why. My husband and I would greatly appreciate your suggestions as to how to effectively pray about this. Thank you!!!*

Liberty's Answer: Some issues are so emotionally charged that they cannot be addressed head on unless some foundational work is done first. This foundational work can be done in prayer.

Regardless of what you read on many Christian web sites regarding homosexuality or deliverance, lesbianism is not caused by an evil spirit! Let me, however, clarify that statement by saying that evil spirits will do everything they can to compound the mistake of making a choice to live in this lifestyle. Deliverance may bring minor relief from harassing spirits who take advantage of this disobedience to God's will. But deliverance <u>cannot</u> fix the wrong thinking and wrong beliefs that led to the individual's wrong choice in the first place.

> *Homosexual beliefs are strengthened by the deceptive hope that the temporary distractions from neediness and pain that may come from practicing such a lifestyle might eventually become permanent.*

When wounded, hurting, fearful, angry men and women are convinced they have to alleviate their own pain, a desperate search for any form of relief can always be justified by their souls. As these individuals' pain gets worse, <u>and it will as no one and nothing but God can ever truly heal it</u>, the enemy keeps ratcheting up promises of ever more enticing choices that will ultimately just drive them deeper into sin and despair.

As we try to cope with some of the harder things of life, we all become aware of behaviors that seem to offer us room to breathe when we feel we are suffocating. Depending upon what "lines were drawn in the sand" (regarding absolutely unacceptable behaviors) when we were younger, we have varying degrees of resistance to different behaviors. Depending upon how clearly we had our gender identity modeled for us as children, we have varying degrees of resistance to the sexual preferences of others. Many deeply confused individuals need to have a new identity imprinting in their souls that only Christ can give.

But until they are prayed into a position of closeness to Him for this to happen, they are in danger of making very wrong choices. Even a dangerous "fix" that brings a temporary sense of false intimacy can seem preferable to the fear that there is no hope of ever belonging or being pain free. This is why some people turn to alcohol, drugs, homosexuality, and other destructive behaviors that they know may ultimately destroy them. At least these behaviors dull the frightening needs and powerful drives within them for a while—and that can seem to be a reasonable trade off from constant pain.

We all know people who have tried unsuccessfully to give up a destructive form of behavior, saying that they asked God to help and He didn't do anything. So why would it be any different if they asked Him again? This is a reasonable question: why doesn't God fix these areas of great wounding and neediness when we ask Him to do so? Because our souls prevent Him from getting close enough to the sources of our pain to heal them.

During our lives, we have all learned how to build strongholds around the wrong behavioral choices that we think help us to cope with things we cannot fix or control. These wrong behavior patterns and thought patterns eventually become hard things in our lives that we don't know how to change.

> *Repeated rationalizations and justifications of wrong choices, wrong actions, and wrong behaviors become addictive thinking patterns.*

Jesus Christ has given us powerful keys to help us strip all of these wrong patterns of thinking out of our souls. Only then will we let Him come into the hidden dark places in our minds, wills, and emotions to heal, deliver, and free us permanently. **All He wants us to do is cooperate with Him**.

Your niece may not have any concept of how to cooperate with God to be healed and made whole. She may have rationalized that she is now finally in a lifestyle that will fulfill her. You will probably not be able to convince her this is a deception until you have laid down a solid foundation of breakthrough prayer on her behalf, which I will get to later.

> *One of the meanings of the word "pray" in the Old Testament is to: stand between, mediate for, and intervene on someone else's behalf.*

Is it not awesome that our prayers can somehow come between another person's wrong choices and the consequences of those sins, as we earnestly request grace and mercy and forgiveness for them? We can't heal them or wash them clean, only Jesus Christ can do that—but we can stand in the gap for them until the grace arrives. We can bind them to the good will of God for their lives until they are willing to accept what Christ will do for them. What a privilege and honor!

Begin to pray the binding and loosing prayers for your niece, starting with the prayers in *Shattering Your Strongholds* (which you say you have). It is very important that you pray these same basic principles for every person in your family. Also pray these same prayers for all of the other people who move in and around your niece's life. This is what I call enacting the "ripple" effect of praying. Sometimes your prayers for someone can be drawing him or her to making a right choice, and another person with a strong unsurrendered soul can pull them off track.

> *Make sure you pray for God's healing and love to reach any person, known or unknown, who is having or could have any influence in her life.*

Pray the binding and loosing prayers in *Shattering Your Strongholds* just as they are written on pages 131, 139, and 171 (changing the 131 and 139 prayer pronouns and other phrases from praying for yourself to praying for others). As you pray, do not focus your prayers on the problem, instead focus your prayers on the solution God is going to bring. Once you are comfortable with the intent of these prayers, then pray them in your own wording—

being sure to pray with pure intent for God's love and goodness to heal and bless. Pray that God's will would be done, not what you think God's will could or should be. Frequently bind your niece's mind to the mind of Christ so that she might continue to hear the thoughts, intents, and purposes He is thinking towards her—even if she is rejecting them at first.

One of my ministry's Directors is a Spirit-filled psychotherapist who has all of his clients pray the prayer on page 30 of *Breaking the Power* for 30 days in a row to help break the soul power within themselves. He says he firmly believes this prayer "marinates" the strongholds and wrong mind sets within each person's soul causing these strongholds to be "tenderized" enough to be easily dismantled. This same prayer can also be prayed for others by praying it as a confession of agreement for their healing. Here is a sample of how to turn the *Breaking the Power* "page 30" prayer into a confession of agreement for someone else:

Lord I want to be a blessing to _____ by praying for your healing and blessing and freedom to come to him/her. I bind _____'s soul to its destiny as a fully integrated, divinely created part of God's plans for his/her life. I loose the wrong beliefs, attitudes, patterns of thinking, control factors, self-centeredness, and layers of deception and denial that _____ 's soul has created to deceive him/her.

I loose the wrong desires and motives that _____ 's soul has used to bring others into agreement with its deceptions. Lord, do not let his/her soul derive power and ungodly satisfaction from any wrong agreements with other human beings. Where this has or may now be happening, please cause confusion and division in any wrong agreements that have been or are now being struck. I loose the power of the wrong agreements that _____ 's soul has already entered into and the soul-ties it has joined together with.

I loose the generational bondage thinking _____ 's soul has received and accepted as fact. Jesus Christ has power to make _____ free from all generational bondage, and I now confess and prophesy that truth over him/her. I bind _____ to the full liberty that Christ has extended to him/her through the giving of a brand-new covenant relationship, new family heritage, and new bloodline that can be (or even now is) his/hers.

Lord, I loose the layers _____'s soul has laid down over the deepest, darkest chambers within itself. I loose the deceptive layers of self-control, self-protectiveness, self-defense, and self-centeredness that have been piled over his/her most vulnerable areas so needful of God's grace. I loose the lies _____'s soul is clinging to. I loose the guilt _____'s soul has tormented him/her with. I loose the deceptions _____'s soul has hammered him/her with and used to cause him/her to cave in to its control.

I bind those persons having any interaction with or influence over _____ to your will. I bind their minds to the mind of Christ. I loose stronghold thinking from their souls, and I loose word curses from them. Lord, heal them and draw them to yourself.

Pour your grace and mercy into_____'s needs and hurts, and into the wounded souls of every person he/she comes into contact with. I bind him/her to your will, the divine plumb line for the truing up of his/her mind, emotions, and will. Let your truth become the straight edge of his/ her life, the guiding light and the backbone of his/her soul. May the day come soon where _____'s soul will rise up and say, Bless the Lord, O my soul, with all that is within you. Forget not His benefits. Remember what He has done for you! In Jesus' name, Amen.

7

FREEDOM FROM SOULISH BACKLASH

Question: *I have just read **Breaking the Power**. Thank you for writing it. It affirms some of the things that the Lord has been leading me towards that I was not paying attention to. I am now praying the binding and loosing prayers almost daily, and I am experiencing a lot of changes! As I have been praying these prayers, I find it interesting that I am no longer interested in sugar. When the idea to eat something sweet comes to me, I have no desire to act on it. I'm so thankful!*

As I study your book, I am trying to pray with all of the new information I am learning. So far I have experienced much freedom. But lately I have also been experiencing some very difficult things like real sadness and heaviness. The other night I woke up feeling like it was hard to breathe. I have also had nightmares, which is rare for me. What is going on?

Liberty's Answer: These are the reactions of your unsurrendered soul as it recognizes that a powerful opposition is beginning to threaten its position of control in your life. Your soul has been protecting many things it has feared to have exposed, and it senses that its hidden "things" are not as safely buried as before. As the protective layers are coming off of these hiding places, your soul is reacting. An anxious soul's first line of defense will often be to throw up mental, emotional, and physical distractions to get you to stop doing what is upsetting it.

The soul begins to telegraph its distress to your body in the forms of nightmares, shortness of breathing, perhaps even mini panic attacks. One of its strongest alliances against your spirit is a wrong mind-body agreement. The further problem here is that wrong agreements always open doors for enemy interference.

From my experience with people who are new to this powerful way of praying, as well as reactions

I have experienced as I prayed these principles, I believe your unsurrendered soul is trying to scare you into giving up your prayer attack.

Most of us are aware that mental anxiety, emotional unhappiness, and fear often manifest themselves in physical behaviors such as nervousness, nail biting, overeating, pill popping, smoking, etc. Fear also prompts a fight-or-flight response in the body (with flags flying and adrenalin pumping) that produces elevated levels of blood pressure, sensitivity to noise, jumpiness, and nervous agitation. Unresolved issues in the soul will often telegraph to the mind various cravings for a physical fix of sugar, alcohol, or drugs. You have already seen a great reduction in what has probably been a past reliance on sugar.

Question (Part 2): *I understand that layers my soul has placed over the areas of my vulnerability are probably coming off because of these prayers. But should I be experiencing such reactions to just getting free? It seems to me I should be doing something to let the Lord get to this distress, shouldn't I? If I just focus my prayers on binding and loosing to remove the layers of self-protection, how do I know if I'm cooperating with what He wants to do?*

Liberty's Answer: You can be assured that you are cooperating with God when you are praying these prayers. You are focusing on getting your soul out from between you and God! The Apostle Paul tells us where to use these Keys of the Kingdom prayers!

> *For though we walk (live) in the flesh, we are not carrying on our warfare according to the flesh and using mere human weapons. For the weapons of our warfare are not physical (weapons of flesh and blood), but they are mighty before God for the overthrow and destruction of strongholds. (Inasmuch as we) refute arguments and theories and reasonings and every proud and lofty thing that sets itself up against the (true) knowledge of God; and we lead every thought and purpose away captive into the obedience of Christ, the Messiah, the Anointed One*

(2 Corinthians 10:3-5, Amplified).

When God has specifically given us the means and the ability to do something big, along with keys and instructions, He has a reason for expecting us to use them. Through the words of your mouth as you are praying the binding and loosing prayers, you are volunteering to surrender your innermost hiding places to God. That is your part. God will be right there with His part. Let me offer another short prayer for you to pray:

Lord, I am determined to keep pressing on towards you. It is not always comfortable exposing my hidden chambers after staying behind my stronghold walls for so long. But I want to be free more than I want to be comfortable. I look forward to being both in the future! Again I bind my will to your will, and I bind my mind to the mind of Christ. I bind myself to the full truth of your Word.

I loose, dissolve, disrupt, and destroy all of the defensive reactions of my soul. I loose the effects and influences of wrong agreements I have been a part of, and I loose the effects and influences *of old word curses I have accepted into my wrong belief system! I loose the residue of the fear and doubt my soul has known. I <u>set</u> my will to receive your healing and your love, Father, and I earnestly thank you for your grace and mercy. Amen.*

8

FREEDOM FROM SMOKING

Question: *While shopping at a Christian supply store, the clerk informed me that a book I had ordered was waiting for me. I hadn't ordered any book, and it turned out to belong to another person with the same last name. Curious, I asked to see the book and it turned out to be* **Shattering Your Strongholds**. *I ordered a copy for myself and have since finished reading it. I found the book to be very enlightening and have recommended it to everyone I know. I have struggled with the stronghold of smoking for over twenty-five years. I desperately want to be free. How do I pray to have this addiction destroyed?*

Liberty's Answer: The first truth to recognize is that your smoking habit is a symptom of something much deeper in your soul. This habit most likely began as an attempt to dull the unrelenting drives coming out of your soul's emotional needs. It has now become a physiological addiction as well which makes it harder to overcome.

You have read my first book, and I now strongly recommend that you go on to the second book, ***Breaking the Power*** (of unmet needs, unhealed hurts, and unresolved issues). It will give you further insight as to what is actually happening within your unregenerated body and your unrenewed soul. Thank God that, as believers, our born-again spirits are just fine! Your goal now is to use the Keys of the Kingdom prayer principles to bring your body and your soul into alignment with the wonderful status of your regenerated, renewed, rebirthed spirit.

As you are praying, bind every cell of your body to the destiny purposes for which God created it. This is something I do every day. Bind every cell of your body to God's will, that they will come into agreement with God's plan for His temple within you.

Loose the wrong mind-body agreements that give your mind the power to link with your body's addiction to nicotine to procure the chemical response the soul wants.

Loose, break up and destroy, the neural pathway from your mind to your body directing it to act out wrong behaviors.

I love your testimony of how you found the first book. Thank you for the encouraging words and our staff will be praying for you.

Question (2nd e-mail): *I can't believe you responded to my first e-mail! Thank you for praying for me and thank you for the encouragement. I have since purchased your second book, **Breaking the Power**. I do understand now how my smoking addiction started as an attempt to pacify an unmet need—it was the need for acceptance and to fit in somewhere. And I do agree that my addiction has gone past "unmet needs" to becoming a physiological behavior. Your books are powerful, God is All-Powerful, and your message is greatly impacting and changing the way many of us think, act, pray, and respond to God. I thank God for what He is revealing to His people through you!*

*Please help me now. I am praying the training wheel prayers, and I am on my way to reading your third book, **Producing the Promise**. I need a training wheel prayer to specifically BREAK, CRUSH, SMASH, DESTROY, AND TEAR DOWN my physical, mental, and emotional* *addictions to cigarettes, smoking, and nicotine. Can you send me a training wheel prayer that I can diligently pray every day for this addiction?*

I so desperately want to be free. I pray. I groan. I throw away my cigarettes and say, "No more," and begin to feel strong. Then I weaken and the battle begins again. I lose every time and feel guilty because of my failure. Then the cycle starts all over again. I have vowed that I would give the cigarettes up. But I keep breaking my vow and I know what the Word says about this, which makes me feel worse! I know how incredibly busy you must be, but I would be forever grateful if you could send me an e-mail training wheel prayer.

Liberty's Answer: It is very important for you to understand and remember that your smoking is just a symptom. There are much deeper issues here. The prayers in *Breaking the Power* regarding unmet needs, even the Preparing for a Mate Prayer (whether you are married or single or not, even trying to find a mate) have some interesting phrases about looking to other people or things (such as nicotine) for relief for your feelings of neediness and inadequacy.

This is not a case of simply giving you a prayer to quit smoking. The smoking is only a symptom that has become an addictive behavior.

The need now is to loose the effects of wrong agreements in your mind and the deception that this behavior addiction gives you comfort and relief that you cannot get any other way. This is the same deception that alcoholics and drug abusers need to recognize as well.

Your soul believes God doesn't care enough to meet and heal your needs and hurts. He does care, of course, and He is quite ready to help you. You should focus your prayers upon loosing, breaking, crushing, smashing, and tearing down your soul's stronghold patterns of thinking. This is the only way you can have the intimacy with Him that brings the deepest of healings.

You must voluntarily remove all *"high things"* that your soul would *"exalt between you and full knowledge of God"* (2 Corinthians 10:3-6). The primary **high thing** here is the stronghold-protected belief that the chemical drug of nicotine is the best way for you to get comfort for your inner turmoil. It is very easy for your soul to convince you that this is true, especially if you have asked God to take away the smoking and you feel that He has not done anything.

Focusing on fighting or outrunning a symptom will never create a way for God to heal the source of the symptom. Even if you manage through determination of your will to stop smoking, the need for some form of coping mechanism to deal with the **still existing source** will only surface in another behavior. This is why many former smokers turn to eating or other coping behaviors. They have "overcome" the behavioral symptom of the smoking, but another coping behavior pattern takes its place.

> *The answer is not to overcome the symptom by sheer will power, the answer is to break apart the stronghold defenses that are keeping God from healing the source. Once the source is healed, you will be able to break the physiological addiction.*

Pray the binding and loosing prayers in both books you say you now have, praying calmly and with confidence and faith. **Stop worrying about and focusing on the smoking!** You need to begin focusing on the **Divine Source** of all help and all answers with as much trust and confidence as you can. Here is the way to cooperate with Him as you pray:

1. **Loose all fretting and worrisome thinking about the <u>problem symptom</u> and your past failure in overcoming it.**

2. **Bind yourself to God's will, loose your soul's resistance to His workings in you, and expect Him to heal the <u>problem source</u>.**

Faith is often described in the original languages of the Bible as *"trust and confidence in the goodness and power of God towards you."* This is a trust that will never be disappointed, especially as you remove your soul's interference with His work of grace in your life. My intercessors and I will be praying with you. Here is a short prayer for you to pray:

Lord, I'm sick and tired of trying to self-medicate my needs and pain with nicotine. I'm sick and tired of my soul's attempts to dictate my behaviors. I bind my body and my soul to your divine plans and purposes for my life. I bind my will to your will and my mind to the mind of Christ. I choose to stop focusing on my symptom of smoking. I choose to stop focusing on the "problem." I choose to focus on your answer. I choose to focus on your ability to heal and my ability to cooperate with you.

I loose all stronghold thinking and wrong beliefs and ideas I have about you taking care of me. I loose all wrong agreements I've allowed my soul to come into regarding the information I've always heard about how hard it is to give up nicotine. Help me to hear what you will be saying to me. Help me to respond to your love with a complete abandonment of self-concern. Lord, I choose to now believe for a great healing in my soul which I know will cause me to be completely free from nicotine. Thank you for everything you've given to me and all that you're going to give to me. Amen.

9

FREEDOM FROM FOOD DEPENDENCY

Question: *Isn't there some means of using these Keys of the Kingdom prayers to help me with my overeating? I'm seeing breakthroughs in other areas of my life, but I am still overeating. I know I shouldn't, but I do. What is wrong with me?*

Liberty's Answer: I understand the struggle with food. In our church functions and fellowship, we can avoid coming into close proximity with many temptations such as alcohol, nicotine, and drugs. But food is at every Christian gathering we participate in, isn't it? Marrying, burying, even tarrying, all culminate in banquets, brunches, and refreshments. So the theory of avoidance isn't very effective with regard to misuse of food. In your heartfelt question above, you almost seem to be quoting the Apostle Paul in his epistle to the Romans:

> *I decide to do good, but I don't really do it; I decide not to do bad, but then I do it anyway . . . It happens so regularly that it's predictable. The moment I decide to do good, sin is there to trip me up. I truly delight in God's commands, but it's pretty obvious that not all of me joins in that delight. Parts of me covertly rebel, and just when I least expect it, they take charge. I've tried everything and nothing helps. I'm at the end of my rope*

(Romans 7:19-23, *The Message*).

He was speaking these exact words for so many of us, was he not? We want to overcome areas of our lives, but we fail so regularly that we begin to think failing again is almost predictable. I especially appreciate how Eugene

Peterson translates the Greek in verse 22 and part of 23 to say, I truly delight in God's commands, but it's pretty obvious that not all of me joins in that delight! Our born-again spirits want to do only the will of God. Our unsurrendered souls want to do anything else!

Quoting from *Breaking the Power*, **"We eat food our body doesn't need for many different reasons. Sometimes we eat just to chemically elevate our moods . . . Sometimes we eat to dull our thoughts . . . into oblivion. Sometimes we eat to compensate for feeling rejected, unloved, or inadequate. Some eat to try to 'fill up' a sense of great emptiness inside themselves."**

Harmless enough, right? Wrong! These misuses of food are not simple forms of self-comfort that can be easily controlled. The body learns to tolerate the chemical breakdown of the foods "used," such as sugar's ability to alter the chemical makeup of your body. This means that the same amount of food as eaten before will be ineffective. As certain foods continue to be "used," the body needs more and more of them to create the same chemical reaction. This causes the dependency upon the food's chemical breakdown to become more powerful.

When we temporarily succeed in "using" food to take the edge off of our unmet needs and unhealed hurts, our minds lay down a neural pathway between the mind and the body. This establishes a powerful mind-body agreement that will be turned to again and again.

> ***When the pain and need in the unsurrendered soul begins to stir and well up once again, the soul remembers its last "fix." The mind-body agreement kicks in and forces our thoughts of comfort food to the forefront of our thinking, powerfully displacing other thoughts of logic and reasoning.***

Unless you know how to break the effects and influences of the wrong mind-body agreements, these thoughts can cause overwhelmingly powerful cravings for the desired food. Psychologists say that we will almost always move towards such dominant thoughts. I say this is probably true, <u>unless</u> you know how to loose the hold of those dominant thoughts and take them captive to Christ (see 2 Corinthians 10:5).

There are a couple of other interesting side effects of the unsurrendered soul's deceptiveness at work here. The first one is that our souls will justify using food to comfort ourselves with the rationale that we deserve something to help compensate for the hard things we have suffered. "If this food gives me a little sense of comfort when I've been through so much, how can that be wrong?" This is a subtle rationale that grows more and more powerful each time it is used.

The second thing I have noticed is how so many people confess a failure to get the victory over a struggle in their lives, and then immediately begin to "beat up" on themselves. "I know I shouldn't have—I felt so bad when I did—I should have been stronger—I feel so guilty—I'm just so weak, etc." I have seen people do this before **failing** a struggle as well as **after** failing a struggle. There seems to be a false sense of bargaining going on here. It is almost as if the soul were trying to show that since it felt sooooooo guilty and bad, shouldn't that atone for some of the failure?

> *Be aware that a lot of mental and emotional stressing over feelings of guilt in the soul does not mean the soul is working on surrendering to God. It only means that it is working to keep up an appearance of trying to do better. It is really much soulish ado about nothing.*

After trying for years to break a pattern of eating in the late evening before I went to bed, I began to test this theory of breaking up the mind-body agreement regarding food. In the late evening when I would want to eat, I would immediately pray and bind my mind to the mind of Christ. Then I would loose the wrong mind-body agreements and wrong directives being sent from my mind directing my body to take some form of comforting action (i.e. **get food!**). These wrong thoughts loomed like huge NFL football players about to crash into the end zone of my mind! So, it really seemed amazing how effective this small prayer was. It worked every time for several weeks, diminishing any desire to eat before going to bed.

Then I noticed an interesting thing happen. I began wanting to eat late at night again. When I recognized the old patterns trying to reestablish themselves, I would prepare to pray the same simple prayer. And guess what? My mind immediately oozed out a weasel message, "No, don't do that. I won't bug anymore you about eating. Okay?" I am totally serious, these are the words that came to me.

I realized that food was no longer the main issue! The main issue was that my soul was trying to negotiate a deal to distract me from praying that prayer. The prayer was obviously intimidating to my soul. But if my soul could con me into not praying that prayer through its sneaky weasel tactics, then it could do an end run around my ability to shatter its influence over my eating.

Such sneakiness makes me really mad, assuming, of course, that I catch my soul in the process of being sneaky. The more I pray these prayers, the more I'm onto its games. I no longer feel any desire to eat late at night. Hallelujah, my soul's score is still "0" on this issue!

Lord, I can't avoid being around food, but I can learn to avoid "using" food for wrong purposes. I want to be predictable in my victories, not predictable in my failures. I want to react to my soul's pain and need with an increased desire to open up all of my hidden chambers to your healing and love. Don't let me forget that physical pain is my body's way of telling me it is in trouble, and mental and emotional pain is my soul's way of communicating its trouble. I bind myself to your will, and I loose all of my saul's efforts to convince me that I am fine. I am not fine, but I'm going to be!

I do not want to be caught in any more wrong mind-body agreements. I loose all such wrong agreements. I loose any and all wrong signals and misdirectives that my mind would try to send out to involve my body in a destructive behavior to create a "fix" for my soul's discomfort. Lord, I will not provide any more "fixes" for my soul. I want to expose the sources of its discomfort for your healing.

I loose all of the stronghold thinking that has deceived me and helped me to deny what I have been doing to myself. I loose all thoughts that come from my soul's craving for anything that will take the edge off of its sources of need and pain. I loose my soul's grip on its wrong attitudes and wrong mind sets about food. I loose my soul's grasp on the word curses spoken to me and about me that it has internalized and called "truth."

I will not be deceived any longer that my soul's guilt and sorrow over my failures are any attempt on its part to surrender to God's will. I will stop focusing on how "bad I feel" about failing and focus instead on "what am I going to do now" to avoid failing the next time. Lord, show me every sneaky trick of my soul, and help me catch its cheap bargaining tactics. I want my soul surrendered to you in every way. I want to be well, and whole, and healthy to fulfill my destiny plans for your Kingdom work. Thank you for caring about me. Thank you for helping me. Thank you. Amen.

10

THINGS ARE UPSIDE DOWN—DOES THIS MEAN THE PRAYERS ARE WORKING?

Question: *I have been praying the binding and loosing prayers for two weeks now. Within the last couple of days, I have been struggling with feelings of fear and insecurity. I have had these and other "old" feelings come up that I haven't felt in a long time. I thought they were long gone. Last night I had the most outlandish, strange dream that I think I have ever had. Is all of this part of the healing process, or is the enemy trying to torment me to get me to stop praying the binding and loosing prayers? I'm sure he is not happy about me uncovering this truth about binding and loosing.*

Liberty's Answer: Bless your heart, I'm glad you wrote to ask about this. Yes, these are "classic" symptoms of the fact that **THE PRAYERS ARE WORKING**! Things are being uncovered that your soul has been able to keep just under the surface of your consciousness, expending great effort and energy to do so. Your soul and the enemy are not happy with you <u>first</u> finding out about this truth of the Keys of the Kingdom and <u>secondly</u>, that you are putting this truth into practice. You are doing serious damage to the deception and denial your soul has been running against you. You are also closing doors that the enemy has been using to take advantage of your soul's denial.

You are experiencing flack from your soul's fears and the enemy's anger, as well as some old unhealed hurts and unresolved issues that are being exposed. But there is no need for you to worry or back off! Fear is only an absence of trust and confidence in the goodness of God towards you. As you pray, always bind yourself to the truth that God is trustworthy, faithful, and good. Recognize that your soul does not trust God for good things for your future. In fact, know that your unsurrendered soul is at enmity with God.

Those who live according to the sinful
nature have their minds set on what that
nature desires; but those who live in
accordance with the Spirit have their
minds set on what the Spirit desires. The
mind of sinful man is death, but the mind
controlled by the Spirit is life and peace;
the sinful mind is hostile to God. It does
not submit to God's law, nor can it do so.
Those controlled by the sinful nature
cannot please God

(Romans 8:5-8 NIV).

The goal of the binding and loosing prayers is that your soul will surrender totally to pleasing God by giving itself to the will of God! Then it will no longer fight for control of your life, instead your soul will learn to "walk in the Spirit." Oh, happy day!

I strongly suggest that you get *Breaking the Power* and begin to pray the prayer on page 30 every day for at least a month. You seem to be getting a strong immediate reaction which means you have some big things on the run. I don't always tell new "pray-ers" to go right for so much meat, but I think if you do, you can take advantage of the scrambling going on in your soul right now.

Take heart in knowing that you have stirred up such distress, particularly on the part of the enemy. This may be the first serious backlash you have ever launched against him and his personal plans to take advantage of your soul's misguided attempts to deal with your old unresolved issues. Yahoo!

Lord, I bind every square inch of my slippery soul to you. I bind my mind to your mind, Jesus. I bind my emotions to the Holy Spirit's balance and healing. I bind my will to your will, Father God. I'm on track with you to the best of my ability. I will take advantage of my soul's confusion at this point and press it to within an inch of its survival.

Soul, I bind you to God's preordained plans to use you as a messenger to the world, as a natural translator of His end times spiritual message to all who will hear. I loose all of your schemes, plans, and soulish agendas that would cause you to try to circumvent such an awesome destiny. You have a much bigger agenda to follow now, so give up your tawdry little plans. Fear not, soul, for you are going to know peace, wholeness, and wonder as God brings you to the fulfillment of why I was born.

Thank you, Lord, for empowering me to become perfectly aligned with you in my spirit, soul, and body!

11

SO THIS IS WHAT HAPPENS
WHEN THE WALLS COME DOWN!

Question (Part 1): *Thank you for being a mentor as I grow into the freedom and strength of Christ. I live in New Zealand and I have been praying the training wheel prayers out of **Shattering Your Strongholds**, binding and loosing specifically as the Lord leads, for the past six weeks. I have ordered your next two books but they have not arrived yet.*

My problem is that the sweet, gentle, kind, understanding, wise, and empathic person that I thought

I was, <u>has gone</u>. In her place is someone that I don't even like very much. This person is forthright, has an opinion on everything and, right or wrong, doesn't hesitate to give it in a loud, authoritative voice. I am so impatient and intolerant now. Maybe I always was, but suppressed it because of my immense hunger for approval.

Liberty's Answer: Your question and your insight into the probable answer is excellent. You have nailed the classic symptoms of someone who (through the binding and loosing prayers) has realized that he or she has been trying to keep an appropriate facade in place to give the impression of being a nice person. And all the while, anger, fear, and pain have been gnawing and scratching away at the back of that facade.

I believe you are seeing an overreaction of an angry, fearful soul that is finally spewing out what it has tried to bury within itself for too long. The binding and loosing prayers you have been praying have stripped your unsurrendered soul of its walls that allowed it to keep its pain and rage fairly under control. This is a good thing, whether it seems like it or not. This is breakthrough! The "out-there-and-in-your-face-attitude" is occurring because your soul is probably thinking something like this:

> *Okay, I can't keep my real feelings down anymore, so I'm going to let them out with such force that it will intimidate anyone who wants to mess with me. I'm a little unsteady about who I am right now. So I have to make sure that it is apparent to everyone that I cannot be pushed around or overpowered, that I am someone who knows how to protect myself. Nobody is going to want to mess with me!*

Question (Part 2): *For most of my life, I was fearful and hid from people. I allowed myself to be used and abused because of a desperate craving for approval from substitute mothers and fathers. Some time ago I lost my temper with a loved one who then died. I vowed never to be angry with anyone again (because they might die and it would be too late to rectify it). Now that safety valve has been shattered, and I find rage welling up and spilling over about things that aren't even my business.*

Liberty's Answer: Wow! God is really showing you a lot about the sources of your stronghold building and He is doing it very fast. That might be scary, but it is also incredibly exciting. God doesn't want you dawdling around with this healing process for an extended amount of time. He wants you healed now! He has obviously planned something for the next step of your destiny that is imminent.

Question (Part 3): *Should I trace the anger back to its real source years ago and ask God to heal the memory? I don't know:*

> *A.   If with all the years of isolation and alienation, I haven't learned how to relate to people in a healthy way.*

> *B.   If this is my real personality and I have to exert more self-control and self-discipline to be accepted.*

> *C.   If I should now bind myself to such things as more mercy, compassion, sensitivity to others, and loose aggression, inappropriate anger, etc.*

Liberty's Answer: You make this easy:

- **A is completely correct,**

- **B is partially correct, as your real personality is trying to come forth. But as I said above, it is trying to come forth with a lot of intimidation being projected to protect itself. A little bit of self-control and self-discipline at this time would not hurt, but only if it is tempered by the Holy Ghost and surrendered to God through constant prayer. Your soul's immediate efforts (if left to its own devices) would be to drive this seemingly unpleasant persona back undercover and replace it with a "phony-but-more-likable" facade again.**

- **As for C, just continue to use the binding and loosing prayers as you are using them. Don't try to fix a process that isn't broken!**

Question (Part 4): *There is an element of bruised pride involved, too. The lovely, "spiritual" person I thought I was, was just a sham and underneath I have just as many bumps and sharp corners as everyone else. I realize that the former "personality" was false, but now I don't quite know what belongs to me, what doesn't, or how to behave with people any more. I feel quite raw and lost and a bit weepy. I feel the Lord's presence and peace deep inside, but there is so much insecurity and unhappiness on the surface level of my life right now.*

Liberty's Answer: Please let me assure you that you are way ahead of so many people. In Eugene Peterson's **The Message**, Psalm 51:16-17 is translated to read, *"Going through the motions doesn't please you, a flawless performance is nothing to you. I learned God-worship when my pride was shattered. Heart-shattered lives ready for love don't for a moment escape God's notice."*

So don't fear, don't back off, and don't worry— God is doing a very quick work in your heart-shattered life.

Do try to watch what you say. But know that if you say something hard or unpleasant while you are trying to let God sort out who you are, the Lord will be right there to empower you to say something like this:

> *"I'm so sorry I did that, or said that, or responded like that. God is doing a new and true thing in me, and I'm trying ever so hard to learn how to cooperate with it. Please forgive me. He's pulled the rug out from under the so-called 'nice' person I used to try to be. And I'm trying to get to the truth of where He wants me to be now."*

You might be amazed at how God will allow grace and mercy to flood over those around you when you do this. Add this short prayer to your other prayers:

> *Lord, I want to be real. I want my soul's pride shattered. I want a heart-shattered life! But I don't want to make life difficult for others as I am getting there. Please cover me with your grace and mercy until I get completely out of my old cocoon. I know I'm acting a lot like a grubby*

grub right now, but I'm moving towards a miraculous change. The awesome hope of that keeps me on track.

I so want to be who you created me to be. I bind myself to the truth of who I am. I bind myself to the paths you have ordained for me to walk. I bind my hands to the work you have ordained for me to do in the work of your Kingdom. I loose all wrong ideas about who I have believed I am and who I wanted to be. I know that my eyes have not seen, nor have my ears heard, the wonderful things you have planned for me. I want it all, Lord. Thank you so much for creating me to be your child. Amen.

Epilogue

I hope you have found answers in these e-mail
dialogues, and that you will find a new measure of peace
and comfort in knowing how your prayers can make a
real difference. As you agree with God's already established
will in heaven, your prayers become like catalysts for the
manifestation of His answers on earth.

*Thus says the Lord, Keep justice, <u>do and
use righteousness (conformity to the will
of God which brings salvation)</u>; for My
salvation is soon to come, and My
righteousness—My rightness and justice-
to be revealed. Blessed, happy, and*

83

> *fortunate is the man who does this, and*
> *the son of man who lays hold of it and*
> <u>*binds himself fast to it*</u> . . .

(Isaiah 56:1-2, Amplified).

The Lord says to *"do and use righteousness."* In the past, I wondered if any but a chosen few really knew how to achieve such spiritual obedience. But, praise God! I now embrace the truth that:

- **we are all chosen,**
- **we aren't few, and**
- **the means of obeying this command are not unknown to us!**

As believers, chosen and loved, our spirits have already **been conformed to the will of the Father—they have been brought into salvation**. Our unsurrendered souls are in the process of being conformed to His will as well. How grateful we can be that Jesus Christ left us spiritual prayer keys to cooperate with this transformation of our souls' learning how to "walk in the Spirit."

I believe we must recognize how self-focused many of our petitions to God have been. However full of faith, so often our prayers of supplication and request are filled with giving God "unknown information" and acceptable options so He will know what to do. The Keys of the Kingdom prayers, when prayed simply and purely, acknowledge that:

- **God knows all,**
- **God can do all, and**
- **God is actively seeking agreement on earth with His answers.**

Our agreement with the will of God (as being the only right answer to every question) brings His best answers into being. What an awesome responsibility and privilege to be so used to make a difference in the world when we pray. Let's embrace and practice Christ's words:

> ***This, then, is how you should pray: Our Father in heaven, hallowed be your name, your kingdom come, your will be done on earth as it is in heaven.***
>
> (Matthew 6:9-10, NIV).

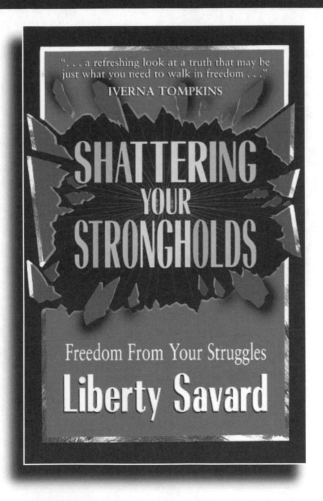

". . . a refreshing look at a truth that may be just what you need to walk in freedom . . ."

IVERNA TOMPKINS

SHATTERING YOUR STRONGHOLDS

Freedom From Your Struggles

Liberty Savard

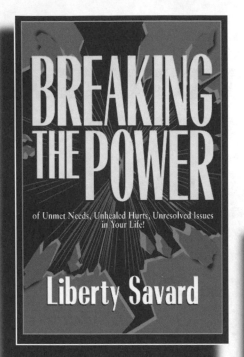

Liberty Savard

You've shattered and broken your strongholds
Now, it's time to begin
PRODUCING
THE PROMISE
Liberty Savard